SURVIVAL

TRUE STORIES

WITHDRAWN

D1441937

Real Tales of Endurance in the Face of Disaster

TOM MCCARTHY

Current titles in the **Mystery & Mayhem** Series

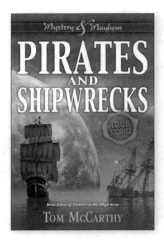

Check out more titles at www.nomadpress.net

Nomad Press
A division of Nomad Communications
10 9 8 7 6 5 4 3 2 1

This book was manufactured by CGB Printers,
North Mankato, Minnesota, United States
October 2016, Job #208075
ISBN Softcover: 978-1-61930-480-2
ISBN Hardcover: 978-1-61930-476-5

Educational Consultant, Marla Conn

Questions regarding the ordering of this book should be addressed to
Nomad Press
2456 Christian St.
White River Junction, VT 05001
www.nomadpress.net

Printed in the United States.

MIX
Paper from
responsible sources
FSC
www.fsc.org   FSC® C008080

Contents

Introduction

Would You Survive?

The most interesting thing about survival stories is that they make you wonder if you could do the same thing. Would you have the smarts, the strength, and the coolness to get out of a tough situation? Could you handle watching your frozen fingers break off in Antarctica or seeing mirages of wonderful cooling lakes while you're dying of thirst in Death Valley, California?

In this book, you won't find boring stories that leave you thinking, "So what? My grandmother could have done that."

Take the tale of Captain Ernest Shackleton, for example. He took his crew on an expedition to the frozen Antarctic in an attempt to cross the entire continent, something no one had done before. But a simple, dumb mistake doomed the plan. Captain Shackleton had to do more than just figure out how to keep everyone alive. He had to make it back home across cracking and shifting ice and raging oceans with roaring winds and towering waves.

Maybe you would have liked to sail with William Bligh, who annoyed his crew so much they threw him and his loyal followers into a small boat in the middle of the vast Pacific Ocean. The men were set adrift thousands of miles from anywhere.

What about trekking with William Lewis Manly on his trip across Death Valley? This is the lowest, driest, hottest place in the United States. It's a long walk, with very little water to be found.

Speaking of deserts, join Mademoiselle Picard on her journey through the desert on the coast of western Africa. After surviving a tragic shipwreck, she and her family faced a long walk to safety filled with perils.

On the other side of the world, Eliza Donner and her family, along with several other families, encountered a different kind of extreme landscape. They found themselves trapped in the snow high in the mountains on their way to a better life in California, fighting for their survival. People today are still wondering how the survivors managed to do just that—survive.

So what do you think? Do you have what it takes to overcome the severest obstacles and make it home safely? Would you survive?

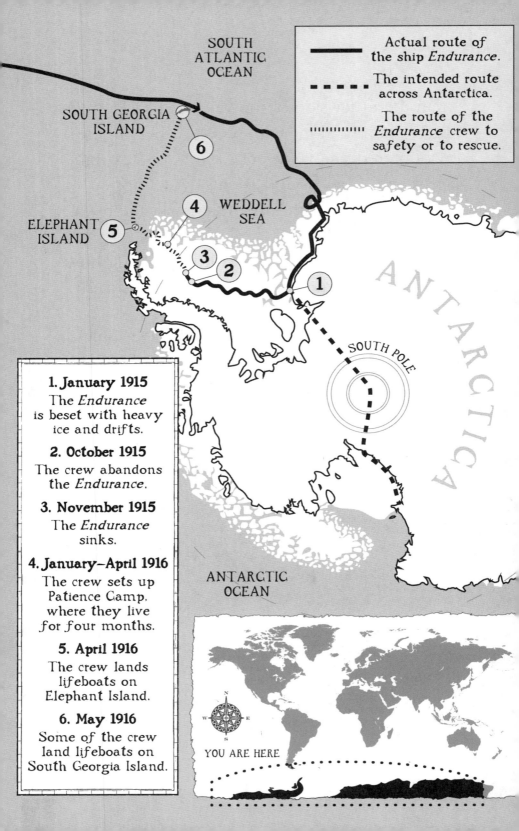

SOUTH
ATLANTIC
OCEAN

Actual route of
the ship *Endurance*.

The intended route
across Antarctica.

The route of the
Endurance crew to
safety or to rescue.

SOUTH GEORGIA
ISLAND

⑥

④ WEDDELL
SEA

ELEPHANT ⑤
ISLAND

③
② ①

ANTARCTICA

SOUTH POLE

1. January 1915
The *Endurance*
is beset with heavy
ice and drifts.

2. October 1915
The crew abandons
the *Endurance*.

3. November 1915
The *Endurance*
sinks.

4. January–April 1916
The crew sets up
Patience Camp,
where they live
for four months.

5. April 1916
The crew lands
lifeboats on
Elephant Island.

6. May 1916
Some of the crew
land lifeboats on
South Georgia Island.

ANTARCTIC
OCEAN

YOU ARE HERE

Chapter One

Escape From the Ice

Men wanted for hazardous journey.
Low Wages, bitter cold, long hours of complete
darkness. Safe return doubtful. Honour and
recognition in event of success.

—An advertisement said to have been placed
in 1914 by Captain Ernest Shackleton for
men to accompany him to Antarctica

The most important question is, why? Why, under any circumstance, in any condition, would someone want to go anywhere with Captain Ernest Shackleton?

The man was quite possibly crazy. He had shown that by putting himself and his crews in the most extreme discomfort for months at a time long before he paid for his latest advertisements in English newspapers in 1914.

At the time that Captain Shackleton might have placed the advertisement, only 10 men had ever stood on the South Pole. Five of those 10 men died soon after, trying to get safely home.

So why?

By 1914, what newspapers around the world had been calling "The Race to the Pole" was over. For years, this race had captured the world's attention as different teams made heroic attempts to be the first to travel to the South Pole, only to fall short of the goal.

Captain Shackleton had been in the race. He had tried to reach the South Pole twice, once in 1901 and again in 1908.

But he hadn't made it.

Captain Shackleton's friend, an explorer named Robert Falcon Scott, also tried to be the first to the South Pole. His expedition was beaten in 1911 by a Norwegian explorer named Roald Amundsen. Robert Falcon Scott and his own team of explorers had been right behind

Roald Amundsen. They reached the South Pole five weeks later and were devastated to see that Norwegian flag whipping in the wind. They had lost.

One member of Robert Falcon Scott's team was so disappointed and exhausted after seeing the Norwegian flag that he simply walked away that afternoon to his death. The last words of Titus Oates were, "I am just going outside and may be some time."

Robert Falcon Scott and his remaining crew would soon join Titus Oates in his frozen death. Shaken, disappointed, maybe even embarrassed by losing the race, they headed back to their base camp. It was hundreds of rugged, almost impassible, miles away. They never made it.

Robert Falcon Scott and his crew had made it to the South Pole, but died trying to return home.

The frozen continent of Antarctica is not an easy place for humans. The air kills you if you are exposed to it long enough.

And the air rarely just sits there.

With very little to block it at the bottom of the world, the wind came at the explorers violently, with great blasts that knocked them off their feet as if they were bits of straw. Plus, the sun in Antarctica disappears for months.

These details didn't make Captain Shackleton any less excited about exploring the continent. He named his 1914 "trip" the Imperial Trans-Antarctic Expedition. Despite his well-deserved reputation for heading up long and painful and frozen expeditions, there was no shortage of men interested in joining him. In his latest plan to cross the entire desolate, frozen continent of Antarctica, about 5,000 men applied for the job!

His goal was ". . . the crossing of the South Polar Continent from sea to sea." He figured the distance to be about 1,800 miles. Some of this would cover ground that had never been traveled before.

Captain Shackleton chose his crew carefully. There could be no cliques, no favorites, no bullies, no friction between the men. They were all in this together from the moment they cast off from England and headed south.

There were 16 Englishmen, four Irishmen, four Scots, and one each from Australia, the United States, New Zealand, and Wales. Captain Shackleton hired seasoned sailors, of course, but also a physicist, a biologist, a meteorologist, a navigator, two doctors, and even an official artist.

The ship, the *Endurance*, was built using the knowledge of all those who had dared to venture into Antarctic waters before. The *Endurance* had powerful engines and a hull made from specially selected pine, oak, and greenhearts. The strong wood could survive the extreme conditions. The *Endurance*, like her name, was meant to withstand anything.

At least, that's what everyone hoped.

On August 8, 1914, the *Endurance* set off from Plymouth, England, heading south. The patriotic Captain Shackleton had offered both the ship and his crew for service in World War I. The new conflict that had started on August 1, beginning the Great World War.

His offer was declined in a one-word telegram: "Proceed." And so he did.

On December 5, the *Endurance* left a lonely whaling station on desolate South Georgia Island. Neither Captain Shackleton nor crew knew that, as the *Endurance* slowly pressed on into the gray and chilled sea off South Georgia Island, it would be a very long time before they set foot on land again.

Two days later, the *Endurance* entered the Antarctic pack ice. This soup of dark seas filled with floating floes of ice could easily crush most ships. Captain Shackleton was careful, though, and the *Endurance* was strong. The plan was to dance gently through the ice and land on Antarctica's coast near the Weddell Sea.

Captain Shackleton wrote, "The Weddell Sea was notoriously inhospitable and already we knew that its sternest face was turned toward us. All the conditions in the Weddell Sea are unfavourable."

They saw the Antarctic coast for the first time by the new year, 1915. The first step of the journey was complete. They were almost there!

Almost does not count.

On January 18, the *Endurance* was wedged in ice, trapped, unable to move anywhere. A small problem, they thought. The crew could wait this out. The ice would shift and the *Endurance* would break free.

Captain Shackleton was concerned though— and for good reason, it turned out. He wrote, "The ice was packed heavily and firmly all round the *Endurance* in every direction as far as the eye could reach from the masthead. There was nothing to be done till the conditions changed, and we waited through that day and the succeeding days with increasing anxiety."

Have you ever spent a night at sea? Falling asleep on a boat is a comforting feeling. The pulsing of the engine is steady and rhythmic. The smooth lapping of the ocean as it rushes serenely by the hull next to your ear drops you to sleep faster than anything.

Imagine, now, sleeping in the same bunk. The engine is silent. The gentle lapping of the water has been replaced with a dull, aching grind. Unexpected groans erupt from somewhere outside as the ice pushes ever closer and tighter. Not so comforting. This is what Captain Shackleton and his crew faced.

They were prepared for the long wait. There was plenty of food and much for the scientists to do while they waited for the ice to shift and free the *Endurance*. June 22 was the beginning of winter in the Southern Hemisphere and soon the total darkness that covered them would end.

The crew decided to celebrate the occasion with a feast.

Captain Shackleton wrote, "To-day the sun has reached the limit of his northern declination and now he will start to come south. Observed this day as holiday, and in the evening had hands aft to drink to the health of the King and the Expedition. All hands are happy. I pray to God we may soon be clear of this prison and in a position to help them. We can live now for sunlight and activity."

They were still trapped two months later.

There is only so much research and exploring of Antarctica one can do when stuck off its coast. Even then, these resolute men were not overly concerned. If anything, they were patient—a quality they would need later.

On September 2, the pressure from the ice made the *Endurance* suddenly shoot up. It came to rest on its side.

This was not a good sign.

The *Endurance,* the solid home these men had depended on for months, was lying down, still trapped in the ice, going nowhere. Worse, it was being slowly crushed. Hope that the coming warmer weather would eventually free it faded.

They had left England a year before and still had not set foot on Antarctica. The situation was grim.

By mid-September, they were running out of fresh meat to feed their dogs. Healthy, well-fed sled dogs were a vital part of the plan for crossing the continent.

On October 27, Captain Shackleton ordered everyone to abandon ship as the groaning ice moved in even more. The *Endurance* would never sail again. Nearly a month later, the end came for that hearty ship. The *Endurance* let out a terrifying series of final groans the men could hear from their camp more than a mile away. The ship was going under.

"We were out in a second and up on the look-out station and other points of vantage, and, sure enough, there was our poor ship a mile and a half away struggling in her death-agony," a crewmember wrote. "She went down bows first, her stern raised in the air. She then gave one quick dive and the ice closed over her forever. It gave one a sickening sensation to see it."

Standing nearby, Captain Shackleton said simply, "She's gone, boys."

An expedition leader must be capable of altering plans, of facing setbacks and responding with clear and precise instructions. Any look of fear from Captain Shackleton, any hint of nervousness in his voice or weakness in his expressions, would have spread like a contagious disease through the crew. Captain Shackleton had a plan. He explained it to his crew, now stuck without a ship in the middle of a frozen nowhere.

"We'll get out of here," he told them. "At some point we will be free of this horrible place."

It was a simple enough sentiment. As long as you don't consider the chances of a small crew of men floating on ice thousands of miles from England, equipped with only a few small boats and no food, facing monstrous, killer seas.

That would have been enough to crush the hopes of anyone but Captain Shackleton. "We will drag our boats to open water, then we will sail," he told his crew.

There was the small matter of the ocean that lay between them and safety. Because there is nothing to block the winds at the bottom of the world, they are always strong. And because they are strong, the sea is always a chaotic mass of nasty currents, enormous waves, and constant spray.

On December 23, 1915, the crew began hauling their three lifeboats—*James Caird*, *Dudley Docker*, and *Stancomb Wills*—across the ice, hoping to find open water.

They were able to go only a short distance. On December 29, Captain Shackleton ordered that they set up camp. They would stay here for four months and name their home Patience

Camp. Keep in mind, they were floating, like tiny specks, on a large mass of ice at the whims of the powerful currents and winds that controlled their frozen lives.

In a January blizzard, they were blown north of the Antarctic Circle. Of course, Captain Shackleton took this as a good sign. He kept up the crew's spirits, even arranging a celebration for leap year day, February 29, 1916. They ate three meals that day, an increasingly rare occurrence.

Captain Shackleton wrote, "The last of our cocoa was used to-day. Henceforth water, with an occasional drink of weak milk, is to be our only beverage. Three lumps of sugar were now issued to each man daily.

"By this time blubber was a regular article of our diet—either raw, boiled, or fried. It is remarkable how our appetites have changed in this respect. Until quite recently almost the thought of it was nauseating. Now, however, we positively demand it."

Here's how starved they were for food—a man searched for more than an hour in the snow where he had dropped a piece of cheese some days before, hoping to find a few crumbs. He was ecstatic when he came across a piece as big as his thumbnail.

Captain Shackleton did not permit panic. Negativity did not and could not exist.

On April 7, the first glimmer of hope slowly emerged on the horizon. They spotted land. It was, Shackleton wrote, "a pleasant sight."

One problem—it was 60 miles away.

On April 9, they took to the sea in the three boats. By then, these boats, which had been dragged across the ice and exposed to the brutal elements, were not in great shape. Still, off they sailed. After seven brutal days being tossed by unrelenting waves and drenched by freezing water, they landed on Elephant Island and dragged the boats up the rocky beach. It had been a very long time since their last walk on solid land.

They had yet to realize that the easy part of the Trans-Antarctic Expedition had just ended. There was still 800 miles of brutal seas to cross—in three fragile boats. Elephant Island was a start, but Captain Shackleton knew they would starve there just as easily as they would have on their barren ice floe.

Of course, Captain Shackleton had it all figured out.

He would take a smaller crew to South Georgia Island to get help. There was that whaling station they had visited at the start of the trip. The rest of the crew would shelter on Elephant Island until they returned. Captain Shackleton figured that the men who stayed behind would have an easier time of it since there would be fewer mouths to feed. In the boat, they'd only need to take enough for six men to last the month.

If they hadn't reached land after a month, they were sure to be on the bottom of the ocean.

This was not a trip taken lightly. But no one wanted to spend another winter in the Antarctic.

On April 24, Captain Shackleton left Elephant Island with five of his crew in the 22-foot *James Caird*. They had reinforced the lifeboat as much as they could. Captain and crew would be at sea for 17 days or more. Would they make it to South Georgia Island, which they had left almost 500 days before?

There was a lot of tension aboard the *Caird* as the crew was pounded mercilessly by heavy seas. Much larger and more substantial ships had been crushed by seas such as this.

With only the navigation skills of crewman Frank Worsley to rely on, they were heading for what was basically a pinprick on a map of a vast ocean. Miss it, and they would continue to sail into oblivion.

If that happened, those left on Elephant Island would also slowly starve and die.

Imagine how the remaining crew on Elephant Island felt. Their companions had to find South Georgia, find a new boat, and return. The odds were not good.

Captain Shackleton did not concern himself with odds. Ever exacting in his planning, Captain Shackleton had loaded the *Caird* with enough supplies to last six men one month. Here's what he packed.

30 boxes of matches
6½ gallons paraffin
1 tin methylated spirit
10 boxes of flamers
1 box of blue lights
2 Primus stoves with spare parts and prickers
1 Nansen aluminum cooker
6 sleeping bags
A few spare socks
A few candles and some blubber oil
in an oil-bag

Food:
2 cases nut food
600 biscuits
1 case lump sugar
30 packets of
Trumilk
1 tin of Bovril cubes
1 tin of Cerebos salt
36 gallons of water
250 pounds of ice

Instruments:
Sextant
Sea anchor
Binoculars
Charts
Prismatic compass
Aneroid

The trip was brutal. They froze, they rowed, they adjusted sails, and bailed. They could close their eyes just for a few moments, only to open them and do it all over again. One mistake and they would be sunk.

On May 10, they landed on the South Georgia coast, right on schedule. They'd made it!

Almost.

They had landed on the wrong side of the island. It was a steep mountain and a crumbling glacier away from the whaling station where they hoped to find help.

Captain Shackleton was exhausted, but he considered the options. They could set off and cross the mountains to the whaling station or spend another winter where they had landed. If they stayed where they were, what would happen to the men on Elephant Island?

In a very Shackleton-like manner, Captain Shackleton pronounced his decision: "We must push on somehow."

On May 19, he and two crewmen began a trek that must have been pure torture. These men were not in good shape. For months, their bodies had been slowly deteriorating, muscles shrinking, strength fading. And now they were asking these bodies to hike across a glacier.

Physically, they were done in, wiped out, exhausted. Their clothes were drenched, their bodies drained. But that did not matter.

There are times when it becomes more important to be mentally fit, to be able to press on despite the pain. The extraordinary suffering they had endured for nearly two years had strengthened them beyond anything any other human could offer.

Captain Shackleton described looking at the mountain that stood between them and safety.

"We were now feeling the strain of the unaccustomed marching. We had done little walking since January and our muscles were out of tune. Skirting the base of the mountain above us, we came to a gigantic bergschrund, a mile and a half long and 1000 ft. deep. This tremendous gully, cut in the snow and ice by the fierce winds blowing round the mountain, was semicircular in form, and it ended in a gentle incline. We passed through it, under the towering precipice of ice, and at the far end we had another meal and a short rest. This was at 12:30 p.m. Half a pot of steaming Bovril ration warmed us up, and when we marched again ice-inclines at angles of 45 degrees did not look quite as formidable as before."

Thirty-six hours of inhuman trekking brought them to the top of a hill.

Captain Shackleton wrote of the moment:

"At 1:30 p.m. we climbed round a final ridge and saw a little steamer, a whaling-boat, entering the bay 2500 ft, below. A few moments later, as we hurried forward, the masts of a sailing-ship lying at a wharf came in sight. Minute figures moving to and fro about the boats caught our gaze, and then we saw the sheds and factory of Stromness whaling-station."

Imagine that moment, the sweet engulfing moment of pure joy that must have flooded over them. Were there whoops of joy? Screams of delight? Certainly those amazing men were elated, but they simply turned to each other and shook hands.

Back on Elephant Island, it had not been easy for those left behind. The winter weather, as they waited for rescue, was, in the words of one crewmember, "simply appalling."

Because of that appalling weather, it took three rescue attempts to get to the shore of Elephant Island. Of course, Captain Shackleton led the rescue group. There was no question of that. It was August 30, 1916, when he landed back on Elephant Island.

As advertised, Captain Shackleton had taken 28 men on a hazardous journey. And he had brought all of them back.

When he saw Captain Shackleton step back onto Elephant Island's rocky, icy shore, one of his men did something that would have been strictly forbidden at any time during the long, painful, hopeless struggle. He cried tears of joy.

Captain Shackleton and his men returned to England and were met by adoring crowds and showers of praise from everyone. Who would not be impressed by what many people still call the greatest survival story ever told? King Edward VII made Captain Shackleton a knight, and he would afterward be known as Sir Ernest Shackleton. The Royal Geographical Society gave him its prestigious Gold Medal. The men who Sir Ernest Shackleton saved with his courage and unwavering strength would love him for the rest of their lives.

For a while, Sir Ernest Shackleton traveled and spoke to large crowds of curious Englishmen who wanted to hear from the hero himself what it was like to survive the Antarctic. But called by the life of adventure he missed, the restless and bored captain returned to the Antarctic in 1921. Sadly, he died of a heart attack anchored off South Georgia. He was buried there, so close to the place where he had earned such fame and respect.

WHAT ELSE IS GOING ON IN 1914?

- The assassination of Archduke Franz Ferdinand of Austria becomes the catalyst for the beginning of World War I, later known as "The Great War."

- The first electric traffic light is installed in Cleveland, Ohio. Previous attempts to use gas-powered traffic lights had ended in explosive catastrophe. Electric lights are a much safer alternative.

- Stainless steel is invented, a huge scientific leap, since it does not rust like ordinary steel.

- Charlie Chapman, the funnyman with a little mustache and a bowler hat, makes his film debut.

- Construction begins on the Lincoln Memorial in Washington, DC.

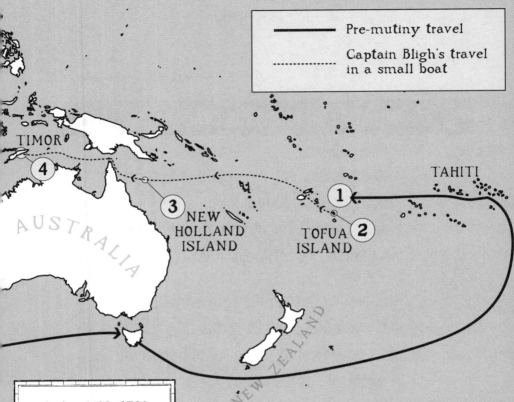

Pre-mutiny travel

Captain Bligh's travel in a small boat

TIMOR

AUSTRALIA

4

3 NEW HOLLAND ISLAND

TOFUA ISLAND

1

2

TAHITI

NEW ZEALAND

SOUTH PACIFIC OCEAN

1. April 28, 1789
Captain Bligh's crew mutinies and forces Bligh and 18 loyal followers into a small boat.

2. April 29, 1789
Captain Bligh and his men land on Tofua Island for fresh water. One of them is killed by native islanders.

3. May 26, 1789
Captain Bligh and his men land on New Holland Island for food and water and barely escape being killed by islanders.

3. June 14, 1789
The small boat makes it to safety in Timor.

YOU ARE HERE

Chapter Two
Adrift in the Pacific

The 19 men crowded in the very small boat
knew that they were going to die. They also
knew, without a whisper of doubt, that their
deaths were going to be slow and painful.
After all, there was very little food in the boat
and only a bit of water to drink. They were
3,000 miles from safety, across a wide ocean.

In a few minutes, the rope that tethered their
tiny boat to the large and comfortable HMS
Bounty would be cut. And then they would
float away.

Their desperate situation was all because of
Captain William Bligh. Only moments before,
William Bligh had been the captain of the
Bounty. His many years of experience at sea
had taught him that a captain's job was to lead

his crew. The captain of a ship is not meant to be anyone's friend. He is supposed to lead and the crew is supposed to obey. That was the way it had always been.

The *Bounty* was in the Pacific Ocean to collect plants for England's colonies. During the long voyage from England to the South Pacific, some of Captain Bligh's crew on the *Bounty* had grown very upset with William Bligh. Secretly, they decided that they had had enough.

"William Bligh curses and swears and punishes men for no reason," they whispered to each other. "William Bligh is a brutal, cruel, and vicious man who never should have been a captain."

The men decided it was time to mutiny.

On the night of April 28, 1789, the group of rebels snuck into Captain Bligh's cabin. They put a gun to his head and a sword at his back. He was ordered to get into the small boat. Anyone loyal to Captain Bligh was ordered to get into the boat, too.

As they pushed him roughly, the rebellious crew told Captain Bligh the situation was his fault. "Good riddance, and if you drown or starve to death or are eaten by a shark, so much the better," they yelled as they took an axe to the rope and let the small boat drift way.

The crew on board the *Bounty* was a bit more sympathetic toward the other men stuck in the boat with Bligh, but not that much. The men who had sided with Bligh must be punished, too.

This left Captain Bligh and his loyal followers in the small boat, which was designed for small errands in calm harbors. It had not been built for long sea voyages filled with frightened men.

Captain Bligh and his men thought about the hot sun. Storms could sink them in the blink of an eye. They knew that even if they were lucky enough to find an island, the people living there would probably try to kill them.

The only man on the small boat whose face did not reveal fear was Captain Bligh. Sure, he worried about the storms and the lack of food and water and the wild islanders who might kill them. He knew they were thousands of miles from safety and that the odds of surviving were very slim. But he would not show any sign of his concern.

Captain Bligh looked around as he settled himself at the back of the small boat and took control of the tiller. He studied the weary, frightened faces of the men who looked to him for comfort. There are 19 of us in a boat built to hold only 15 safely, Captain Bligh thought to himself. There is no cover from the hot sun. We have very little food and water.

I just need to keep these men alive.

He knew that if his calm face betrayed any sign that he was worried, every man in the boat would fall apart. He began to study the charts he had slipped under his shirt as the rebels had hustled him from his room onboard the *Bounty*. He knew that confidence was contagious. If he acted confident, the men in the boat would feel confident, too.

When he looked up from the charts, he saw huge, black clouds forming ominously in the distance. The sea around the small boat began to crash. A storm was about to hit them.

I hope I can do this, he thought to himself.

As the dark clouds opened and the sky exploded with rain, the winds picked up and the small boat rocked. Captain Bligh quickly ordered his men to cover up the food to keep it dry. They would need that food, what little there was—150 pounds of bread, 16 moldy pieces of dried pork, 6 quarts of rum, 6 bottles of wine, and 28 gallons of water.

Captain Bligh formed a plan as the small boat rolled in the heavy seas. Everyone held on for their lives as water crashed in. He would steer them to the small island of Timor, more than 3,000 miles away. There were English settlers on Timor. It would be safe.

Along the way, they would have to stop at an island or two to get food and water. When they stopped, they would have to take their chances that the people living there would not kill them. There were plenty of islands on the way to Timor, but the people who lived on them were known to have welcomed uninvited visitors in a most unwelcoming way.

Such as beating them to death with stones and clubs.

Captain Bligh steered through the wind and rain toward the closest island, Tofua. He could already see it in the distance through the clouds. Tofua was easy to spot because its high volcano stood out starkly against the dark sky. Once on land, they could stock up with water and get organized for the long voyage to Timor.

Unless the Tofuans bashed their heads in.

They landed on Tofua the next day, April 29, and pulled the boat up the sandy beach. Captain Bligh sent five men to look for water. Two hours later, they returned with three buckets full of fresh water they had found in some small holes. The water was green, but drinkable.

Captain Bligh took charge of the food right from their first meal. He had to be careful that they did not eat up their meager supplies too quickly. Each man received a small piece of bread and a sip of wine. That would turn out to be one of their better meals on the long trip, but they did not know it at the time.

The men needed to get off Tofua before the natives found them, but the storm still raged, making it impossible. The waves crashing on the beach were too large.

As the 19 men crouched nervously on the beach, waiting for an opening, swarms of mosquitoes attacked, making the men miserable. They swatted, hid, jumped up and down, but nothing worked. Compared with what they had to face later on, the mosquitoes were nothing.

Three days later, the men were still waiting out the storm. The Tofuans, by then, had learned of their English visitors. The islanders crept closer, surrounding the stranded men. Every day, they moved a little closer down the beach.

Captain Bligh decided they would have to leave, no matter the weather. He ordered his men to pull the boat into the rough surf. As they headed to sea, he looked back at the beach and discovered that, in the confusion, one man had been accidentally left behind. Captain Bligh and the others stared with open mouths as John Norton was surrounded by islanders.

As the boat pulled away from the beach, the crowd began beating John Norton with stones, dancing around him and celebrating his painful death. Safely out to sea in their small boat, Captain Bligh and the men sat silently, mourning the violent loss of a good friend.

After that, Captain Bligh knew he would have to avoid stopping at islands as much as he could. But there were thousands of miles to go! At some point, they would have to take their chances again. As they made it safely to sea, they all said a prayer and each ate a small piece of bread.

It began to rain so hard that the men couldn't see the man sitting next to him. With the rain came waves that crashed into the little boat and drenched everyone. They grabbed whatever they had and began to bail. They used buckets, hats, and small cups to scoop water up and chuck it out. It was exhausting work, especially on empty stomachs. During that dreadful night, whatever hope they had began to fade.

The rain gave them water to drink, but it also chilled them to the bone. It threated to ruin their shrinking supply of food. The stormy weather was torture, especially at night, when the darkness seemed to swallow them up.

Gloomy, frightening thoughts came at night.

But they continued through the storm, inching toward Timor. On May 14, the sun broke through the clouds. In the distance, William Bligh spotted an island, ringed by mist. Graceful birds flew peacefully over the island. The birds reminded the men of tasty Christmas dinners at home in England. Was it safe to try to land there, Captain Bligh wondered? Should I take a chance? He decided against it, tempting as it was.

By May 18, food was running low. So was the hope of the men on board. They had been at sea for more than two weeks, and the relentless rain seemed as if it would never end.

As the day began to dawn, Captain Bligh looked at his men, worried. He realized that some of them were close to dying. They sat weakly in their seats, barely moving. No one had slept and they had eaten nothing but damp and moldy bread.

They seemed to have given up, Captain Bligh thought. I have to do something.

He steered toward an island where birds flocked over a reef. He held out a bit of bread to tempt a bird to land on the side of the boat. It worked! Two men quickly grabbed it and wrung its neck. They ripped raw meat from the dead bird and Captain Bligh took charge of passing it out. They ate everything but the feathers. Then, in celebration, Captain Bligh allowed the men two spoonfuls of rum and an extra piece of bread. That wonderful meal was a brief and shining moment.

It did not last.

They were hit by a fresh storm with strong winds and heavy sheets of blinding rain. The weary crew was always wet, and the salt water that splashed roughly over them made their skin red and puffy with sores. Their clothes were beginning to fray. They hadn't slept at all. Everyone was afraid of the darkness. They were exhausted.

On May 25, after almost a month a sea, a small bird the size of a pigeon landed on the boat, unaware of what was about to happen. A man quickly caught it and Captain Bligh divided it into 19 small portions. They ate quickly, devouring the tiny strips ripped from the carcass as if it were a grand holiday meal.

As they ate, Captain Blight noticed clouds on the horizon. Was land nearby? He pulled his charts from under his seat, where they sat in a bag to protect them from the unrelenting rain. He realized they were near the island of New Holland. If he didn't land there, his men would die. He turned the boat toward the clouds.

The next morning found them outside the reef ringing New Holland. Captain Bligh pulled hard on the tiller and pointed the boat toward shore. In the distance, he could see the shore and, beyond that, a thick jungle.

As they rounded a small point of land jutting out into a smooth blue bay, Captain Bligh dropped the anchor. Peering at the deserted shore, he looked for signs of people. He saw nothing that alarmed him. He didn't know if there were people on the island. And if there were, he did not know if they would be friendly.

But it didn't matter anyway. His crew was hungry and dying.

Captain Bligh pulled up the anchor and headed for the beach. As they stepped onto land for the first time in weeks, the exhausted men found hundreds of oysters on the rocky shore. Cracking them open on the rocks in a frenzy, they ate raw oysters with great delight.

As it grew dark, Captain Bligh decided they would stay on the beach. The men had all had enough of life at sea in a small, cramped boat. They tried to build a fire, but the wood was too damp. Despite the lack of a fire, they all slept well anyway, forgetting for one night that they were still far from Timor.

They even forgot to worry whether they were surrounded by natives who would kill them the next morning.

When the men awoke, rested for the very first time in many weeks, the entire group felt happy, their faded hopes refreshed. We will survive, Captain Bligh thought, as he sent out a few scraggly men to look for food. It wasn't long before they returned to the beachside camp with more oysters and buckets of fresh water.

But thoughts of enjoying an island paradise were quickly dashed. Everyone began getting sick. Their stomachs erupted with great pains from gorging themselves on raw oysters, or maybe it was from the mysterious fruit they'd found on the trees at the edge of the beach. Some men became so dizzy they could not walk.

Captain Bligh knew if they were attacked by natives, there would be no hope. They were too weak to fight. They would all be killed.

That night, they made a stew of oysters over a fire. Each man was given two full cups. They would need the energy and nutrition for the final push to Timor.

As they slowly and reluctantly loaded the boat the next morning, Captain Bligh noticed a crowd of natives in the distance. Perhaps the fire from the night before had attracted the unwanted attention. The islanders who emerged from the jungle held long, sharp spears. Captain Bligh became very nervous. He ordered his men to pick up the pace as they worked to load the boat.

The native people began to move closer, forming a circle around the Englishmen on the beach. They began to chant something Captain Bligh and his men did not understand.

Was it a chant of death, a song sung before a killing?

A native beckoned to William Bligh, as if to say, "Stop what you are doing and join us." William Bligh was having none of that. As he shook his head no, more natives with spears joined the circle surrounding him and his men.

They began to move closer.

The men frantically pushed the boat down the beach and into the waves. The circle of chanting natives rushed to stop them, throwing their spears as the boat pushed out to sea. Narrowly escaping with their lives, the relieved crew cleared the reef.

The small boat once again at sea, Captain Bligh knew he had used up all of his luck. They would have to make it to Timor with no more island stops. He said a silent prayer.

As the days passed at sea, the stormy weather continued. The men were starving again soon enough, their skin again raw and burned from the sun. All that remained of their food was a few dried oysters and clams.

Captain Bligh grew sick for the first time, though he tried not to show it. He knew if he complained, even in the smallest way, his men would think that the end was near.

Captain Bligh knew he was the one fragile thread of hope his men had left.

This pain and the torture cannot last much longer, he thought. We need to reach Timor soon or we will all die.

On June 12, Captain Bligh noticed clouds on the horizon, signaling that land was nearby.

He checked his charts. The island wreathed by the clouds in the distance could very well be Timor. Once there, he would face one more challenge. To get to Timor, he had to get the boat over the dangerous reef surrounding the island and through the crashing waves. Even so, Captain Bligh was jolted from his despair by the sight of his destination.

He checked his charts one more time. He was sure—it was Timor in the distance.

As the sun rose, Captain Bligh pulled hard on the tiller and pointed the boat and its weary crew toward shore. For the first time in 41 days of pain and intense worry, there was hope on the horizon. By the end of the day, they were so close to the land that they could smell its freshness and its promise of safety.

The next day, Sunday, June 14, Captain Bligh ran the boat through the dangerous waves breaking over the reef. He gleefully passed the last hurdle that could have sent them all to the bottom of the sea.

As the boat glided into the calmer water off the friendly shore, Captain Bligh was overwhelmed. We have arrived, he thought to himself. We have completed a remarkable voyage. We have spent 46 days and sailed 3,400 miles in the absolutely worst conditions men should have to face. We are safe.

As if to second Captain Bligh's thoughts, two cannons from the village fired off welcoming blasts to the small boat filled with men.

Captain Bligh's incredible journey to bring his men to safety in such a small boat is still considered the most amazing tale of navigation ever. But was the mutinous crew of the *Bounty* right when they said he was a mean and unfair captain?

English ships returned to the South Pacific and captured the crew on the *Bounty*, who were brought back to England in chains. Their trials caught the attention of the entire country. Some were hanged for their roles in the rebellion.

Later, William Bligh was appointed governor of New South Wales in Australia, where his strict rules soon angered residents. They rebelled. Sound familiar? William Bligh, still considered by many to be a remarkable hero, returned to England. He would never again be given command of a large expedition or an important job. Almost 175 years later, after many popular movies and books about the famous mutiny on the *Bounty*, people still wonder about William Bligh.

WHAT ELSE IS GOING ON IN 1789?

- The first novel written and printed in America, *The Power of Sympathy* by William Hill Brown, is published in Boston, Massachusetts.

- The United States Electoral College unanimously votes George Washington as the first president of the United States. John Adams becomes his vice president.

- Revolution is in the air in France, as the National Assembly is declared, women march on Versailles, and public dissent against the monarchy grows.

- It didn't come in a blue box back then. Thomas Jefferson introduces the macaroni machine to America.

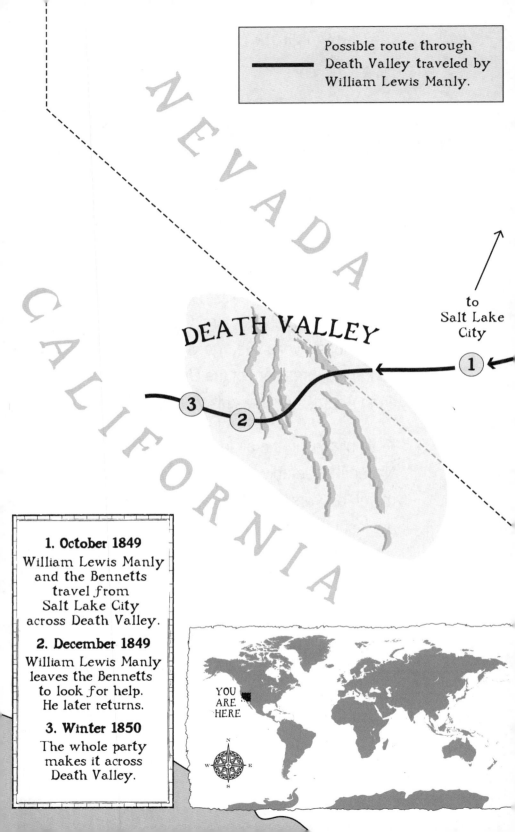

Possible route through Death Valley traveled by William Lewis Manly.

NEVADA

CALIFORNIA

DEATH VALLEY

to
Salt Lake
City

1

3   2

1. October 1849
William Lewis Manly
and the Bennetts
travel from
Salt Lake City
across Death Valley.

2. December 1849
William Lewis Manly
leaves the Bennetts
to look for help.
He later returns.

3. Winter 1850
The whole party
makes it across
Death Valley.

YOU
ARE
HERE

N
W   E
S

Chapter Three
Lost in Death Valley

As a young boy growing up in Vermont in the 1820s, William Lewis Manly fell in love with stories about the Wild West. He was spellbound. These strange and exciting tales sang to him in mysterious ways.

If you headed out West, you'd find vast riches and wide open spaces. There were dangerous animals so wild and so big that they could eat a man for breakfast and be hungry again before lunch. There were even wilder men who had been living in the mountains and the deserts for so long that they forgot what it was like to be civilized.

William Lewis Manly heard stories about mountains so high that no one could travel over them. He learned about the air in the desert that sucked up moisture for miles around, leaving nothing but dry pain and misery for anyone who had the misfortune to try to cross.

Deserts, he heard, were so hot, the sun could blister a man's skin.

Those stories were a magical and powerful song to young William Lewis Manly. He could not get them out of his head. This was a boy who could not sit still. His parents knew that. His neighbors knew that. His teachers certainly knew that. They constantly had to tell the boy to sit still and stop daydreaming. It didn't do any good, though. Once he heard the song of the West, he was never the same again.

He told everyone he had Western Fever.

When William Lewis Manly was just nine years old, his father hitched a horse to the family wagon, lifted the boy up to the seat, and said goodbye. William Lewis Manly drove that wagon by himself for hundreds of very hard miles. He went all the way out to Michigan to claim land for a new family farm.

That dangerous trip was just the beginning of his rambling education, and it made the child's Western Fever even stronger.

Western Fever came very close to killing William Lewis Manly more than once, but he kept going. By the time he was 20 years old, he was a strong and seasoned traveler. He had learned there were only two rules—some men survived and others did not.

Living off the land by hunting and trapping, William Lewis Manly moved farther West. Once, he shot a buffalo and ate a piece of meat raw, right off the bones. His leg was gashed by a flying axe and he spent nights frozen in snow drifts. He lived through encounters with deadly snakes and fought crazy men who wanted to kill him for a bowl of soup.

Traveling across the wild frontier of the United States made William Lewis Manly a very wise man.

During a trek through Wisconsin, he once got so sick he thought he would die. Lying in his tent in the damp forest, barely alive, he dreamed of the West. "I'd rather live on the top of the Rocky Mountains and catch chipmunks for a living," he told a friend, "than to live here and be sick."

While in Wisconsin, he had met another hunter named Asabel Bennett. This man and his wife, Sarah, took William Lewis Manly in and fed him when he was sick, and they all became very good friends. As William Lewis Manly recovered, they talked about moving West. It turned out that Asabel Bennett and his wife had Western Fever too. When William Lewis Manly recovered enough to travel again, he left their homestead with promises to meet again, maybe under the huge western sky.

Western Fever changed to Gold Fever in 1848.

That's when James Wilson Marshall found some gold nuggets in a small stream near a sawmill in California. Soon after that, the entire country became crazed for gold and the instant wealth it promised to bring. People all across the country heard the news and packed their bags, thinking about a better life in California. News of gold nuggets the size of his fist lying in the mountains of California made William Lewis Manly's head snap up.

I'm going to California, he thought, and I'm going now.

In Wisconsin, Asabel Bennett thought the same thing. Very soon, the Bennetts and William Lewis Manly would meet again.

William Lewis Manly quickly learned that the trip to California would be more difficult than any other trip he had made before. In the West, mountains were higher than any he had seen. Rivers flowed faster and seemed impossible to cross. As he approached Utah, he discovered the deserts. These flat, barren stretches of hot sand looked like an alien landscape to him.

Lost in a winding canyon outside Salt Lake City, William Lewis Manly experienced heat so intense that he felt as though he was going to melt. After six days with little food, he began to think he would have to shoot his horse and eat it.

Luckily, he emerged a day later from that twisting canyon onto a large trail covered with the tracks of wagons and horses. As he rode on, he saw a large encampment in the distance.

At the edge of the camp, he counted more than 400 people, all heading West.

With a sense of relief, William Lewis Manly stopped and set up his tent. He was happy to find so large a group of people with Gold Fever. Through the night, he sat with some men and talked about the gold in California and what they would do with it.

As the sun began to slowly rise the next morning, William Lewis Manly noticed a man walking by. He jumped up in amazement when he recognized the man. It was none other than Asabel Bennett, his friend from Wisconsin.

They greeted each other with shouts of glee and talked of their journeys to this place in Utah, so far from Wisconsin and still so far from California.

William Lewis Manly told his friend how difficult his long trip had been. Asabel Bennett's trip had been even harder, more so because he had his young children with him. There had been an outbreak of cholera that had killed dozens of his friends. He talked about gunfights and how Gold Fever had made men crazy.

Thoughts of gold and California had turned some men violent, Asabel Bennett told his friend. By the time the two friends sat and talked by the fire that evening in October 1849 outside Salt Lake City, Asabel Bennett was very tired and very frightened.

"Get us to California, my friend," he pleaded. William Lewis Manly agreed.

"I will help you," he said.

In the large camp of 400 people with their fat oxen, horses, and wagons, everyone was making plans. It was late in the year, too late to try to cross the mountains safely, but no one wanted to stay through the winter in Utah when there was gold in California.

Some planned to take their wagons south to California on a route around the mountains called the Spanish Trail. Others argued that the Spanish Trail was too long and would take too much time. They would go north and take their chances in the mountains, hoping they could get through before it snowed.

William Lewis Manly and the Bennett family decided to play it safe. They went south with the group on the Spanish Trail. Dreams of California filled their heads as they set off. One behind the other on the narrow trail, they looked like a slow-moving train. If it all went well, they would be finding their own gold nuggets before winter.

For some, these dreams would soon become nightmares.

The first two weeks of travel on the Old Spanish Trail were easy, but slower than most of the travelers wanted. People were getting impatient. One night, as some restless travelers complained about the slow pace, a young man rode into camp with a map that he said showed a shortcut. It would save them hundreds of agonizing miles.

William Lewis Manly was nervous about this shortcut. He did not know the young man with the map and did not trust him.

Something did not seem right.

No one had ever tried the shortcut before. Another man in the group agreed with William Lewis Manly. He said to the others, "If you want to try that way, fine, but I believe you will get into the jaws of hell."

The Bennetts did not want to listen to that warning. They had young children and needed to get to California as fast as they could. They told William Lewis Manly they wanted to take their chances on the shortcut. Since he had promised to help, William Lewis Manly went along with them.

But he did not feel confident about the decision.

Survival

It took only one day for them to get lost. The mountains grew higher and the trail narrower. The new map with its shortcut was wrong. A day into the trip, the group found itself on the edge of a high, gaping canyon. There was nowhere to go. They slowly edged themselves away from the dead-end cliff.

That night, the young man with the map snuck away from camp while everyone slept. He was never seen again.

The next morning, sitting on the edge of the canyon, many of the travelers realized the map with the shortcut was a lie. It took three days to turn the wagons around and start to look for another trail to California.

They had to get away from the mountains. Winter was approaching fast. In the mountains, winter meant snow and snow meant death. Most of them felt foolish about believing in the stranger and his map. Most of them decided to try to catch up with the group that had headed out on the Spanish Trail.

Not everyone made this choice. But they should have.

Twenty wagons decided to keep going on, including the Bennetts. They continued to believe in the shortcut. The Bennetts asked William Lewis Manly to help them and he felt obligated to agree.

As they continued West, the plants and trees disappeared. The land turned barren and the temperatures rose. For some reason, distances were hard to judge in the dry air. Water was becoming scarce.

William Lewis Manly decided to scout ahead for the best way forward. Walking in front of the wagons, he climbed the brown, rocky hills and looked for the best path to follow. Sometimes, he was gone two or three days at a time, often with little food or water. Water had become more precious than gold.

And they were lost.

William Lewis Manly came to a frightening realization: The only water he could find was high in mountain streams, but the wagons could not travel high in the mountains.

The situation looked hopeless, and he wished briefly that he had not promised the Bennetts that he would help them. If I was by myself, he thought, I would be in California by now. I'd be counting my gold.

The small band traveled slowly, and each day their misery grew. Their clothes became ragged and the sun scorched their skin. Their throats were so parched they choked on the dust and cried out for water. Even deer and rabbits stayed away from the heat and horrible dryness.

This made hunting for food impossible.

One afternoon, William Lewis Manly, who was ahead of the group as usual, climbed a hill and saw a high mountain range in the distance. Below the peaks there was a flat valley. That is where we have to go, he thought.

As he stood trying to figure out what to do next, William Lewis Manly began to cry softly to himself. He had not done this since he was a boy. He thought about the Bennetts and their innocent children and he was overwhelmed at the thought of what lay ahead.

There was no choice, he would lead them through the valley and they would try to make it to California. But how, he wondered?

I will go first, he decided, and learn the route. Then I'll return to save these poor lost people.

At this point, they had been traveling across the desert for nearly two months since leaving the Old Spanish Trail. Their oxen were weak and thin from lack of food and their wagons were battered and falling apart. Everyone was weary and discouraged.

The small wagon train of hungry men, women, and children, pulled by starving oxen, could barely make it a mile. Everyone knew that if they kept moving this slowly, they would all die horrible deaths.

William Lewis Manly told them he was leaving to find a safe way out of their miserable predicament. "Stay here and be safe," he said. "I will find a route through this hellish place and I'll come back and help you."

They could only hope he would return.

As he left, William Lewis Manly said a silent prayer to himself. Please let these poor, unfortunate people still be alive when I get back.

If I make it there and back.

It took him 26 days to make it to California, memorizing the trail along the way. The desperate group waited patiently. They had no other choice. They killed an ox for food, though by then it was so thin there was little meat. Months had passed since their stomachs were close to being filled. The meat was tough and stringy and tasted strongly of the bitter sagebrush the ox had been eating.

Still, it was enough to keep them alive as they waited. Asabel Bennett ventured out to find what little water there was dripping under boulders in dried streambeds. They kept the children from the sun and tried to keep their hopes from fading by talking of the gold they'd find in California.

Meanwhile, William Lewis Manly made it to California, walking more than 250 miles. What would you do after barely managing to survive a desert crossing? In William Lewis Manly's case, he gathered some supplies and turned right around and walked back into the desert.

He had to save the lost wagon train and his dear friends, the Bennetts.

On the way back, he worried. Would they still be alive? Would thirst and hunger have claimed the lives of the Bennetts and the others he had promised to help? His dread made William Lewis Manly hurry.

Finally, he neared the place where he had left them. He didn't see them anywhere. Had the worst happened? Were those poor families and those innocent children lost forever in such a horrible place, with no food, no water, no hope? The thought was almost more than he could stand.

He found the body of a man lying across the trail. The dead man's arms were outstretched, as if he had been praying for water in his final moments. He looked withered and worn. Later, William Lewis Manly nearly stumbled on the dried, desiccated body of a dead ox. It had shrunk to half its size from lack of water and food.

William Lewis Manly took his knife from his belt and cut a large chunk of flesh from the ox's left leg. It was not much meat, but it was better than nothing.

He ate it raw, devouring it in minutes.

Then he moved on, praying the Bennetts and the others had not met the same fate as the man in the trail or the ox.

As his hopes were fading, he spotted the ragged camp up ahead. They were still alive— but just barely. The Bennetts and the others managed a great sigh of relief and even a feeble cheer.

There were no tears of joy, though. No one had enough moisture left in their bodies to make tears. Everyone drank from the canteens of water that William Lewis Manly had lugged with him, but there was barely enough for everyone to get even a few sips.

William Lewis Manly looked around and saw nothing but misery and worry. Even after drinking from the canteens, Sarah Bennett and her children cried out for more. But there was nothing more to give them, not even a drop.

William Lewis Manly took charge, as only he could.

"We will move ahead," he said, "and cross this horrible valley." Crossing the parched valley would not be easy. Everyone was too weak to withstand many more challenges—this was their last chance. The group abandoned their wagons, which were so dilapidated they could barely roll anyway. Whatever could not be carried was tossed into a pile to leave behind. They knew they could travel much faster without things to weigh them down. Time was running out.

They took only a single ox, and on it they hung cloth slings to carry the children, who by then were far too weak to walk.

As they began to creep away from the camp that had sheltered them for so long, everyone was silent, lost deep in their own thoughts. In front of them, heat waves shimmered in the distance like mournful signals of what lay ahead. Was it death or salvation? Some were too tired to care.

There was no water anywhere. The group was desperate, but didn't dare waste any steps trying to find some. As they moved slowly ahead, the heat nearly paralyzing them, they came on what looked like a spring bubbling from the dry, brown earth. The water tasted horrible, but they drank what little they could scoop out with their hands, taking their chances they would not become sick. As nasty as it tasted, the water was appreciated. But they still had no food.

William Lewis Manly fought to keep up the spirits of the pioneers. He told them what was waiting for them in California if they could just keep moving ahead. "California is only a short walk from here," he told them. "There are green and rolling hills with flowing streams of sweet and endless water. There are fruit trees and cool breezes. Just keep going."

He painted wonderful pictures of what he had seen in California. His stories of water and cooling breezes and juicy oranges and apples seemed to work. He noticed that if he stopped talking about the richness that waited for them in California, people became sad and silent and stopped moving.

His encouraging stories were interrupted twice on the slow trek through the valley. They found the dried skeletal remains of a man who seemed to have dropped right in his tracks, trying to take one more step. Then, a mile farther, they found another body, this one better preserved. William Lewis Manly recognized him as someone who had started out with the large and hopeful group in Utah.

It was an eternity since they had left Utah so full of hope for gold and good fortune. Now, the hopes of this man lay dried and withered on the desert floor.

Each time they found a body, the group stopped and stared, thankful they were still alive, even if just barely.

They moved on toward a mountain range they could see in the distance to the north. Mountains meant streams and water and animals to hunt. Those mountains in the distance meant life and freedom. William Lewis Manly made sure they kept moving, one painful step at a time. He did not stop his encouragement.

Soon, the travelers spotted something ahead that they had not seen in weeks. There was a hint of green standing out wonderfully against the brown landscape that had wrapped around them for so long. Green meant water! It was a wonderful sight, and it pulled them along more than any encouragement William Lewis Manly could provide.

And then they were standing on the edge of the first gentle hill that would lead them from this horrible place. William Lewis Manly smiled for the first time in what seemed to him like forever. It was a startling smile and it was in great and happy contrast to the tears he had shed weeks before.

He turned to his ragged group and heard someone say as she looked back, "Goodbye, Death Valley." The name would stick.

Soon, the group stopped at the most beautiful sight, more beautiful than any gold. Water, cold and crystal clear, danced over the rocks in a wide stream running from the green hills. It gurgled like laughter as it flowed downstream. And it whispered the sweetest song these weary travelers had ever heard.

Survival

After leading his friends to safety, William Lewis Manly settled down and bought 250 acres of fertile farmland in the Santa Clara Valley, near San Francisco. In 1862, he married Mary Jane Woods and they led a quiet and prosperous life.

Accounts of his efforts to keeping his party of desperate friends together in Death Valley spread slowly. In his later years, his stories made him a popular and interesting speaker.

Today, if you tour Death Valley, you will find three places named for William Lewis Manly. There is the Manly Beacon near Zabriskie Point, Manly Peak in the south between Panamint Valley and Death Valley, and Lake Manly, which is mostly dry during the year—as it should be in a place called Death Valley.

WHAT ELSE IS GOING ON IN 1849?

- France issues its first postage stamp, eight years after the United Kingdom introduces the concept.

- Elisabeth Blackwell becomes the first female doctor in the United States—an extraordinary achievement considering the level of sexism she had to fight to pursue her medical training.

- Minnesota becomes a territory of the United States of America.

- Zachary Taylor takes the oath of office and becomes the 12th president of the United States of America.

- The Hungarian Revolution comes to an end, with the Hungarian revolutionaries defeated by the combined forces of Austria and Russia.

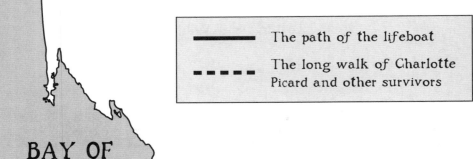

The path of the lifeboat

The long walk of Charlotte Picard and other survivors

BAY OF ARGUIN

① →

②

ATLANTIC OCEAN

WEST COAST of AFRICA

SENEGAL

③ Saint-Louis

1. June 1816
The *Medusa* shipwrecks.

2. One day later
Charlotte Picard's lifeboat lands on the coast and the group begins to walk to the town of Saint-Louis.

3. Eight days later
They are found by rescuers from Saint-Louis.

YOU ARE HERE

Chapter Four

The Two Trials of Mademoiselle Picard

On June 17, 1816, a large sailing frigate named the *Medusa* left France. The crew and passengers of the *Medusa* were bound for new and exciting lives in the French colony of Senegal, Africa. Senegal is a country that juts into the Atlantic Ocean above the equator on Africa's west coast.

The *Medusa*'s captain thought he would have an easy voyage. He was inexperienced and didn't bother to prepare for emergencies. There were only six lifeboats, not nearly enough to carry the 400 passengers to safety if anything happened. There was no extra food. There were no barrels of fresh water to drink in an emergency.

The captain should have done more to prepare.

It turns out the *Medusa* was cursed. The 400 people aboard did not realize it until the ship crashed into a reef 30 miles off the West African coast. The ship quickly began to break apart.

The hopes of everyone on board the *Medusa* sank as fast as the ship itself. Pieces of the shattered wooden hull floated away in the Atlantic Ocean. The frightened passengers began to panic. On the deck, 18-year-old Charlotte-Adelaide Picard watched nervously with her family. In the distance, she could see blurred and hazy waves of heat rising over the horizon from the vast Sahara Desert of Africa.

Some people aboard the *Medusa* had already drowned when water rushed in suddenly and trapped them below the deck after the crash. Charlotte Picard watched the bodies drift away in the early morning light.

Charlotte Picard gazed at the heat waves drifting skyward from the Sahara. Land was near. She thought if she and her parents and brothers and sisters could escape the doomed ship and make it to land, they would be safe.

But appearances can be deceiving.

Charlotte Picard soon learned two things. First, getting away safely from the madness that had descended so quickly on the sinking *Medusa* would be very difficult. Second, endless miles of boiling desert would test her strength and will to survive as much as the wild ocean breaking the *Medusa* to bits around her.

As the *Medusa* crumbled on the reef, desperate survivors showed their worst behavior. Fights broke out over food and small casks of water. Angry passengers demanded places in lifeboats and shoved others aside.

Charlotte looked to her father for help. He remained calm and told her not to worry. We will be fine, he told her. But she could see the tension in his eyes and knew he was only trying to comfort her.

Order and politeness and decency broke apart faster than the disintegrating *Medusa*.

In the confusion on the *Medusa*'s deck, an officer came up with a plan he thought would save everyone. He ordered a group of men to build a large raft from pieces of the *Medusa*'s shattered hull. Charlotte Picard watched as the frantic men built a ramshackle raft 60 feet long and 20 feet wide, tying it with rope that had raised sails only a day before.

In the panic, the officer in charge did not notice the threatening clouds creeping slowly over the doomed ship until it was too late. Soon, darkness blanketed the uneasy group as the storm blotted out the midday sun. Then, the clouds burst open, unleashing a violent squall that pushed enormous waves over what remained of the *Medusa*.

Charlotte Picard thought her life was over. She watched helplessly as a woman and her baby were washed overboard, then crushed by a towering wave. She heard only a scream, then silence.

The sea became very rough and the wind blew with great violence and force. The *Medusa* shuddered. Charlotte Picard heard a stream of confused cries rising from passengers. As night approached, the storm's fury worsened. Waves ripped the *Medusa*'s hull. Water poured in.

Those who could still stand knew it was time to abandon the shattered ship. Fights broke out at the rail. Everyone wanted to jump into the lifeboats when the time came. People fought for their lives. Nothing else mattered.

Soon, panic washed over the deck more powerfully than the waves. As the lifeboats were lowered, survivors fought for seats as the *Medusa* groaned and sank deeper onto the reef. No one wanted to trust their lives to the shabby raft that had been built so hastily.

Standing beside Charlotte watching the madness overcome passengers, her father refused an order to take his family to the raft. He called out to the officers in the lifeboats, pleading for seats. One by one the boats were rowed away, the crews ignoring him. In desperation, Mr. Picard grabbed a pistol and pointed it at the officer in command of the last lifeboat.

"I swear I'll kill every one of you if you don't let us on your boat!" he screamed over the wind.

The officer relented and Charlotte, her parents, brothers, sisters, and a cousin climbed down from the trembling *Medusa* and crowded aboard. There were 46 people on a lifeboat built to safely carry 20.

While the Picards watched from the lifeboat, 146 men and one woman boarded the raft. Its deck dropped below the surface of the sea from the weight. Some of the men stood with water up to their knees as the raft was tied to a lifeboat. The raft had few supplies and no way to steer it to the coast. The officer in charge planned to tow it to the coast with the lifeboats.

As the fragile ocean caravan began rowing to shore, Charlotte Picard watched as people on the raft fought for space. Some were thrown into the sea to make room.

The first night, the lifeboats and the heavy raft slowly made their way ahead. A young woman on the raft tried to cut some flesh from her dead husband's body and eat it. She had gone mad. She was thrown into the sea and drifted away, still alive. An angry group cut off the head of another man when he tried to steal some extra bread.

Charlotte Picard and her family watched through the night as one man after another was tossed from the raft. By morning, 20 men and the woman had been killed. As the sun rose hot and piercing over the horizon, the boats towing the raft were going nowhere. The raft was too heavy. Everyone would die trying to get the raft to shore.

So the raft was cut loose and its passengers were left to their own fate.

Charlotte Picard and her family had other things to worry about. Their lifeboat leaked and they were still 30 miles from shore. What extra clothing they had was rolled up tightly and stuffed into cracks.

By noon, the heat was so intense Charlotte Picard felt like her head might explode. Hot and steady winds from the Sahara blew fine sand into their eyes and ears. It was difficult to breathe. Each anxious passenger had six biscuits to last until they reached land.

Worse, they were so thirsty that they could think of nothing else. Their throats were so parched they could not swallow and they could barely talk above a whisper.

That night, a second storm hit them. Charlotte Picard worried that the overloaded boat would not last. Bluish clouds streaked across the sky and darkened to the color of copper.

Charlotte Picard heard a sudden screech of wind as waves crashed over the boat. Everyone was horrified by thoughts of drowning, but they kept those thoughts to themselves. The boat was completely silent as the terrible storm raged. The silence was interrupted only by the occasional cries of petrified children. Charlotte Picard watched as a weeping mother tried to comfort her dying baby.

They had only two small cups in the lifeboat to catch the rain. Even with so much pouring down they still had little to drink. Charlotte Picard's younger brothers and sisters begged for water. Charlotte feared her youngest sister would die if they did not get to shore and find water. Charlotte's father, so distraught by his children's suffering, wanted to cut a vein in his arm to give them some moisture, even if it was blood.

Another man talked him out of it.

By the next morning, the storm had pushed the boat close to shore. Charlotte Picard could hear waves breaking on the beach. Everyone was exhausted. There was no water left to drink. They had eaten the last of the biscuits. They worried the boat would be crushed when they tried to row through the crashing surf.

There was no choice but to take their chances with the waves and get to shore.

The crew summoned what was left of their strength and began rowing frantically onto the back of a wave. The lifeboat was lifted and sped quickly to shore, surfing ahead of the white water. As the waves broke over their backs, sailors jumped into the sea and carried the young children and babies to the beach and set them down on the hot sand. Charlotte and the adults climbed wearily from the boat and waded to shore.

They were finally safe from the storm, with solid land under their wet and withered feet. They were free of the terrors of the sea. But 200 miles separated them from the safety of Saint-Louis, where other French people lived. They would have to walk.

From the beach where they rested, they could see a narrow strip of jungle. Was it home to leopards, lions, and poisonous snakes? Beyond the jungle lay the unforgiving Sahara Desert. In the jungle and the desert lived natives who might be watching even as the nervous group sat on the beach. Were they friendly?

The beach ahead was blocked by boulders and jagged cliffs that ran to the sea. The jungle was thick and held many dangers. They knew the fastest way to travel was in the desert, as horrible as that seemed. There was no easy way to Saint-Louis.

The survivors knew that some of the residents of this lonely African coast were friendly and wise in the ways of the desert. They might even help guide the shipwrecked survivors to safety.

But sitting on the beach, relieved to finally be off the terrible sea, they also knew there were people who would kill them on sight. The problem for the travelers would be knowing the difference.

Charlotte Picard realized they had gone from one bad situation to another.

After a brief rest, the group moved inland to find water. Less than a mile away, they noticed grass spouting from a tall sand dune and began to dig. Water soon bubbled to the surface. It was foul-tasting and warm, but they all drank heartily and thought it was the best water they had ever had.

Barefoot, their clothes in tatters, they sat by the makeshift well for two hours, drinking as much as they could. Then, it was time to move on, though they were not exactly sure where they were going—only that they had to head to the south. With soldiers carrying the youngest children on their shoulders, they marched along the coast on the edge of the creeping Sahara Desert. The sand burned their bare feet and they moved slowly.

The second night out, Charlotte Picard spotted an antelope, but it leapt into the narrow strip of jungle before anyone could shoot it.

Too bad, because people were hungry.

By the third day, the officers began to complain that the children were slowing everyone down. If they were abandoned in the vast and empty Sahara Desert, no one would ever know.

Charlotte Picard's father was outraged at the thought they would be abandoned. From his belt he drew a sharp dagger that he had taken from a dead man on the *Medusa*. He walked to the officer who had complained and bought the dagger to his throat. "You are a coward," he shouted. "Slow down for my children."

Two officers drew their swords and surrounded Charlotte Picard's father. Charlotte and her sister stepped between them before any blood was shed. Everyone calmed down. They marched on, sand scorching their bare feet like hot coals. They rested often. Climbing the dunes at the edge of the beach, they found wild purslane, a bitter tasting wildflower. They devoured clumps of it quickly.

"It's the best thing I ever ate," Charlotte Picard told her sisters.

At night, on the dunes that were still burning from the day's intense sun, they could hear the roaring of leopards and lions all around them. They slept fitfully, worried they would be eaten.

Charlotte Picard told her father that the heat reflecting off the bright sand reminded her of opening an oven door after baking bread. It nearly knocked her over. They stopped frequently under trees separating the beach from the Sahara, seeking refuge in the shade. It did little good.

They felt they would suffocate.

One afternoon, a soldier returned with his shabby boot filled with water. He had found it by digging into the sand. He offered the boot and its contents to Charlotte Picard. She drank it gratefully. Water was more precious than food. Water meant life.

On the sixth day of their walk to Saint-Louis, a man in the group headed inland to find water. He returned in less than an hour, panicked. He had seen some tents, a group of tethered camels, and a camp of natives. The weary travelers faced a life-or-death decision. Should they go to the camp? Were these the tents of friends who would welcome them or of enemies who would quickly kill them?

They decided to take a chance. As they arrived at the edge of the camp, the people looked up in surprise. Soon, Charlotte Picard heard much shouting in a language she did not understand. The travelers, worn and ragged, were a curious sight, no doubt.

Charlotte Picard and her sisters and the others were quickly surrounded by dogs and children. Some of the children threw sand in Charlotte Picard's sunburned face. Others pulled at her sisters' hair. The dogs nipped at legs and women emerging from the tents spat on Charlotte Picard's mother.

Then, a tall, bearded man in colorful robes stepped from the largest tent in the center of the camp and yelled something to the women and children. They became quiet immediately.

Even the dogs settled down.

The man appeared to be the leader of the group, or at least a man everyone obeyed. The man said something else and the women pulled wood from canvas sacks near the camels and built a fire.

Charlotte Picard and her family and the others settled down after the rude introduction to the camp. They began to relax. It had been a wise decision to come to the camp after all. The hostility at the beginning changed quickly to enthusiasm and kindness and a great deal of sympathy. They all looked horrible by that point, burned by the sun, thin from lack of food, bleary-eyed from exhaustion and worry.

The families in the camp fed them milk and lamb and allowed the survivors to quench their thirst from goatskins filled with water. The native children, curious at these odd-looking strangers, stared and cleared places for them to sit and rest.

They made a comfortable bed for Charlotte Picard from cushions and thick quilts. She dropped onto them, exhausted. For the first time in days, Charlotte Picard slept through the night, no longer afraid of lions and leopards.

The next morning, the weary group set out again. The energy from the food and the rest of the previous night faded before noon. As she walked, Charlotte Picard's feet were torn by prickly shrubs sprouting from the sand. Briefly, nearly dozing as she staggered, she became lost in brambles that shredded her dress. When she returned to the group, her feet and legs streamed with blood.

As they plodded slowly along, Charlotte Picard began to notice that the harsh and unforgiving geography was slowly changing. In the distance, she could see hills rising from the brown flatness. On the hills were small islands of green. The temperature began to drop ever so slightly.

With that change, the group returned to the seashore, buoyed with hope that they were making progress. As they emerged onto the beach, they saw a ship sailing slowly past. Had it been looking for them?

Had word of the *Medusa*'s horrible fate reached the outside world?

Charlotte Picard's father grabbed a rifle from one of soldiers and tied a white rag to it. He waved it frantically over his head. The ship slowed, then turned toward the beach. Men on the deck tossed an anchor into the shallow water. A boat was lowered and soon sailors from the ship had landed on the beach with a small stock of food and drink.

Charlotte Picard smiled for the first time since the wreck of the *Medusa*. She glanced at her sisters. They smiled, too.

The crew from the ship left quickly after delivering the life-saving provisions. They would notify authorities that at least one group from the *Medusa* had survived, they said. Relief and gratitude washed over Charlotte Picard.

But the happiness of the moment ended almost immediately.

She saw in the distance a group of men approaching on camels at great speed. The men were dressed in flowing native robes. Charlotte Picard's heart sank to her stomach, then rushed to her throat. Had they suffered so much for so long only to be killed by these angry men?

She looked to her father, standing on the beach. He reached behind his back and pulled his dagger from his belt. Charlotte Picard felt as if she would faint and drop to the sand in a heap. To have come so far and yet fail, she thought to herself.

The fierce-looking men came to an abrupt halt in front of Mr. Picard, who stood his ground, hand on his dagger. The camels groaned as they knelt on the sand. The leader of the men removed the hood that had protected his face from the blowing sand.

He looked at Charlotte Picard's father and smiled.

"Beneath this Arab costume is an Irishman come here to help you," he said. He explained that news of their plight had reached the authorities in Saint-Louis. He had been sent to bring them to safety.

Recovering from their fright, Charlotte Picard and her father reached out and hugged the mystery man. Then, they showered the man with thanks and yelled to the others what they had just heard. There were many tears of happiness as the weary group stood on the beach. At the moment, it seemed like years since the *Medusa* had wrecked.

The Irishman told them that he had arranged for a camel caravan to take them to Saint-Louis. The camels were about a mile away, the man said. He gave them biscuits and told them to rest. They still had a way to go, he said.

"I will bring the camels and we will soon be on our way."

He was back within an hour. Charlotte Picard and her mother looked at the camels and thought the animal was the ugliest beast they had ever seen. The camels returned their stares and groaned. They smelled horrible and were bad-tempered to boot. It seemed safer to walk.

Soon, they reach a small river cutting through the thick jungle. The urge to drink still overwhelmed them after so much time in the heat. As Charlotte Picard and her mother forded the shallow river, they bent to drink but quickly spit it out. They were still too close to the sea and the water was salty.

On the other side of the river, the Irishman called the caravan to a halt and said they would sleep there for the night. We will be safe for one more day, he told them. That night the jungle came alive with the roars of leopards. They did not bother Charlotte Picard in the least. She knew she was safe.

The next day, refreshed, relieved, and extraordinarily happy, Charlotte Picard and her family crossed the Senegal River. She marveled at the trees and laughed at the hummingbirds, red-birds, and parakeets flitting joyfully through the cool air. The grateful group descended a hill to cross a crystal-clear stream that gurgled over bright rocks.

Charlotte Picard knelt at the edge of the bank and drank for a long, long time.

Charlotte Picard and her family settled down in Senegal after their ordeal in the Sahara Desert, but things did not get any easier. The Picards would face disease and near starvation while they struggled to live in the poor and inhospitable landscape. Their hopes for a better life never happened. After two hard years, they gave up and returned to France.

In 1824, Charlotte's account of what happened on the *Medusa* and how she and the others had survived became very popular with French readers. As a result, Charlotte herself became a famous writer, admired by many for her courage and strength.

She later married and settled into a comfortable life in France, never to return to Africa.

WHAT ELSE IS GOING ON IN 1816?

- Mount Tambour erupts in Indonesia, blanketing the world in sulfur and causing global cooling to the point that the following year is known as "The Year Without a Summer."

- Indiana is admitted as the 19th state in United States of America.

- Mary Shelley, while telling ghost stories with Percy Shelly and Lord Byron, comes up with the idea for her famous story of Frankenstein.

- James Monroe wins the presidential election, becoming the final Founding Father of the United States of America to serve in the office of the president.

CANADA

OREGON
COUNTRY

UNRECOGNIZED
TERRITORY

IOWA
TERRITORY

③

④

Sutter's
Fort

②

①

Independenc
Missouri

M E X I C A N

P O S S E S S I O N S

UNITED
STATES

PACIFIC
OCEAN

Area
Claimed
by Texas

REPUBLIC
of TEXAS

GULF
OF
MEXICO

1. May 1846
The Donner Party
leaves Missouri.

2. July 18, 1846
The Donner Party
follows Lansford
Hastings off the trail.

3. November 1846
The Donner Party
has to stop to camp
for the winter.

4. April 1847
The last surviving
members arrive
at Sutter's Fort.

YOU
ARE
HERE

N
W E
S

Chapter Five
A Most Horrible Journey

George Donner was thoughtful and calm. His kindness and fairness impressed everyone who met him. He never did a thing without carefully weighing the good and bad and sorting it out. People said he always made the right decision. People loved him—and no one loved him more than his young daughter, Eliza.

He was so friendly that even people who barely knew him called him "Uncle George." It was no surprise that George Donner was chosen to lead an expedition of pioneers to California in 1846. The journey tested him and his followers like nothing any of them had ever been through.

Even today, many decades later, people still argue about what happened to George Donner and his hopeful group at the end. The story became as twisted as the long trail they tried to follow to California. Eliza Donner said one thing and defended her father. Others tell a darker and more gruesome tale.

To know why, you have to understand that in 1846, the young United States was stirring with excitement. Thousands of pioneers were on the move. California was calling. Stories finding their way back East made California sound like paradise. There were sweet breezes and gentle sun and soil so fertile it would grow anything you planted in it. There was so much free land that a farmer could walk for days on his own property.

George Donner wanted to go, and he talked some neighbors into going with him. Even his older brother, Jacob Donner, was caught up in the excitement. Thirty-two people decided to head west with George Donner for better lives.

When they left Illinois for the perilous trip in April 1846, Eliza Donner and everyone else did not have a care in the world. George Donner was in charge.

There was one problem. No one was quite sure how to get safely to California. There were deserts and mountains and dead-end trails where blasting heat and deep, impassible snow waited to kill unprepared pioneers.

To learn why people still talk of what became of "the Donner Party," it is best to start from the beginning.

George Donner was a great planner, and he planned the entire trip down to the last detail. He had heard it could take as long as six months to reach California. He bought extra harnesses and axles and yolks in case something broke down. He picked special cows known to produce more milk than others. He brought watch dogs and good saddle horses.

Thinking of the fertile land where they would settle, he packed seed and plows and farm equipment. That was not all. He told his wife and children to bring bolts of cheap cotton prints, red and yellow flannels, bright-bordered handkerchiefs, glass beads, necklaces, chains, brass finger rings, and earrings to trade with the Native Americans. They would meet people along the way and it would be a good way to make friends.

The Donners and their friends left Springfield, Illinois, in nine sturdy wagons pulled by strong and hardy oxen. Moving through the waving tall grass of the Great Plains, they looked so much like ships at sea that people called them prairie schooners.

The Donners were in high spirits.

The prairie was so flat and easy to travel over that they covered 14 miles a day all the way to Independence, Missouri. This was a meeting place for hundreds of wagons heading west to California. They arrived on May 10, just as George Donner had planned.

In Independence, the Donner family bought more food and joined a larger group headed out on the Oregon Trail. California seemed close as they moved on. The idea to move to California seemed brilliant to everyone in the happy group.

The difficult part of the trip had not begun.

By June 16, the Donners had covered 450 miles. Things could not have gone better. Eliza Donner's cousin wrote to a friend back in Springfield that she was "perfectly happy."

That was just before George Donner heard of a man named Lansford Hastings. This fast-talking swindler was a man whose first and only interest was making money. Lansford Hastings claimed to have been out West a number of times. Supposedly, he had discovered a faster route, a shortcut, that he claimed was better than the Oregon Trail. It would take weeks off the long trek. He even named it after himself: "The Hastings Cutoff."

Then Lansford Hastings wrote a letter and paid men to ride out onto the trails and give it to the pioneers who were slowly making their way West. For a small fee, he wrote, I will take you to my shortcut. Anyone interested should meet him at Fort Bridger, Montana.

If people want something badly enough, you can sell them anything.

George Donner wanted very badly to get to California as fast as he could. Lansford Hasting's promise sounded like just the right thing. On July 18, near Little Sandy River, Wyoming, George Donner and his group split from the others, who decided to ignore Lansford Hastings. They said goodbye to George Donner and continued on the known trail to Salt Lake City, Utah. This is where everyone knew the difficult part of the trip would start.

George Donner turned left, thinking that, with the Hastings Cutoff, they would get to Salt Lake City first. There were 200 miles still to go to reach Fort Bridger, Wyoming.

Things would never be the same again.

A week later, the Donner Party pulled expectantly into Fort Bridger, a small and ragged outpost on the edge of the wilderness. Lansford Hastings was not there to lead them to his shortcut as he had promised.

A friend of Hasting's was waiting though, and he told George Donner to follow a trail where they would meet Lansford Hastings. Then, they would be shown the way to make the rest of the easy trip to Salt Lake City. The friend said they would find plenty of water and grass for the animals along the way to meeting up with Lansford Hastings.

It was all a lie, but George Donner did not know that it until it was too late.

The Donner Party left Fort Bridger with 20 wagons. Things began to deteriorate almost immediately. Down the trail a bit, they found a note nailed to a forked stick that was jammed into the dry dirt at the edge of the trail. The note was blowing in the wind and it was from the elusive Lansford Hastings. The note said that the trail ahead was too steep and rocky to travel on without help. It instructed them to stay where they were until he could return to help. Lansford Hastings never showed up.

Weary and disappointed, George Donner turned the wagons around. They would have to backtrack through the rugged Wasatch Mountains to Salt Lake City. Following Lansford Hastings had already cost them 18 days. After they reached Salt Lake City, they still had to cross a desert and climb over the tall and forbidding Sierra Nevada Mountains before the first snow in November.

The trip to Salt Lake City was challenging. The trip across the desert to reach the Sierra Nevada Mountains was much, much harder.

For the first time, the group felt tired and overwhelmed. They stopped briefly outside Salt Lake City to gather their strength. On August 30, the Donner Party, now 87 weary men, women, and children, began a treacherous trek across the Great Salt Lake Desert. They were losing the race to beat winter in the Sierra Nevada.

While he organized for the next part of the trip, George Donner checked the supplies they had left. He became very alarmed but tried not to show it. He saw that they did not have enough food to reach California. Feed for the cattle was gone and the water casks were nearly empty. Overhead, the ruthless sun felt like it was burning them right down to their bones.

The trail ahead was barren and brown and filled with deep sand traps that could swallow a wagon whole. The woodwork of all the wagons shrank and cracked in the intense heat.

A sense of anguish grew as the Donner Party looked ahead at the brutal desert.

As they began the trip into the desert, Eliza Donner's mother gave the children small bits of sugar with a drop of peppermint to distract them. But it did little good. Eliza Donner noticed that the adults seemed wearier than they had ever been. For the first time, she noticed just a trace of sadness on some faces.

The once strong oxen that had pulled their wagons so heartily on the Great Plains stumbled and fell. Men went off in search of water and returned carrying pails filled with nothing but desert dust. Cattle dropped in their tracks, dead or unable to walk. The Donners simply left them there to die, withering in the heat.

One morning, as Eliza Donner watched in wonder, a Native American on a fast pony swooped down and killed 21 head of cattle, sending his arrows whizzing through the air. The stunned pioneers could only stand by their wagons helplessly.

Tempers flared as the strain of desert travel grew. John Snyder and James Reed got into an argument after one criticized the other for the way he treated his oxen. Offended by the criticism, John Snyder cracked James Reed on the forehead with the butt of his bullwhip, splitting it open and drawing blood. Angry, James Reed pulled a knife and jammed it deeply into the other man's chest, killing him.

The two men had been friends since Illinois.

Some of John Snyder's family and friends demanded that James Reed be hanged for his act. Instead, George Donner banned his friend from the group and sent him away. He was last seen by members of the Donner Party heading toward the west.

He might have been the luckiest member of the ill-fated group.

Another man simply disappeared into the desert, leaving his wife and children to their own fates. He'd had enough.

Things continued to deteriorate as another man, exhausted and bleary-eyed, accidentally shot his brother-in-law as they sat in a wagon. Still, George Donner kept everyone together, trying as hard as he could to keep spirits up.

As the animals grew weaker, George Donner realized it would be easier on them if everyone walked. They would need the animals to be strong when they reached the Sierra Nevada Mountains.

As they left the relative comfort of the wagons, one of the oldest pioneers, a man named Hardcoop, found to his dismay that he could not keep up. His feet were bloody and swollen. He begged the others for help but they left him beside the trail. He was last seen sitting under a large sagebrush, sobbing.

As they approached the Sierra Nevada Mountains in late October 1846, winter was dangerously close. They were on the edge of the most difficult part of the journey. The last 100 miles of the rugged mountains had dozens of peaks higher than 12,000 feet. Because the mountains are close to the Pacific Ocean, the high peaks trap moisture from the sea.

That's why the Sierra Nevada Mountains get enormous amounts of snow.

Food and hope were running out for the Donner Party, but they decided to go on. California was close. They moved very slowly and hoped it wouldn't snow. What there was of a trail was so steep the weary oxen could not pull the heavy wagons for long. They stopped often. Three oxen died in one day after too much strain.

On one steep and rocky climb, the axle on George Donner's wagon snapped. Trying to fix it, his brother, Jacob Donner, accidentally gashed George Donner's hand with a sharp chisel, cutting it right to the bone. George Donner felt it was a minor wound compared with what they faced and thought nothing of it. He cleaned his hand, wrapped it in a bandage, and fixed the axle.

Then, it began to snow. And it did not stop for days.

George Donner pulled the group together. The oxen were tired, the people drained, and spirits were low. With the snow still falling, the mountains in front of them were impossible to climb. They towered forbiddingly over them. George Donner decided they had no choice but to stay where they were for the winter.

One man, Charles Stanton, said he would take a group and ride ahead, scout a route, and maybe find more supplies. He tried, but in the end, he was stopped by the snow and could go no farther.

As the challenging year of 1846 came to a close, the Donner Party faced the realization that they would have to suffer through the winter high in the mountains.

They set up two camps 10 miles apart, one at Alder Creek and the other at Truckee Lake. Both camps were more than a mile above sea level. Trapped by the growing drifts of snow, they used whatever they could to build shelters.

The stranded people in the two high camps had one thing in common: They all faced weeks of horrible suffering. The weather would not improve for four very long months, maybe more.

Men, women, and children would have to huddle together in shabby cabins, lean-tos, and tents and take their chances.

To protect the 21 people with him, George Donner and his group hastily made tents, taking canvas from the wagon tops and cutting poles from nearby pine trees. Up the trail, the second group made three cabins from pine logs. George Donner's tents were frail and open to the battering of winter winds. The log cabins 10 miles away were cramped. Roofs made from the hides of dead oxen spread loosely over frames made from branches leaked.

Life was miserable for both parties. Food ran out quickly as the snow mounted. The piercing wind bit through their thin and worn clothes. On November 29, 1846, the last of their oxen was killed for food.

Hope was dying as the snow piled higher. Soon people began dying as well.

The first to go was Jacob Donner, George's brother. He had been sick and could take no more. George Donner looked at the body of his dear brother and thought back to Illinois and how he had persuaded him to come along. He felt responsible. They buried Jacob Donner in a snowbank.

Next to die was Joseph Rhinehart. Then James Smith and Milton Elliot, whom Eliza Donner described dying "like a tired child falling asleep."

It was all becoming too much to bear.

They made do with what they could. Men dug through the snowbanks to find what was left of the bony and weary cattle that had died in camp. There was nothing left of them. By the time they had died, they were nothing but bones.

There was no meat left on the cattle to sustain the frantic and hungry survivors. But the men pulled the bodies of the cattle from the drifts and cut out the bones, then boiled them to make a thin, watery gruel.

Eliza Donner and her sisters learned to look for field mice that came into the tent to escape the cold. They flattened them with rocks, then ate them. Peeled bark from nearby trees was eaten, too. They found twigs and dead leaves blowing across the high snow drifts and chewed on them, hoping for anything that would end the cravings in their bellies.

A woman killed her family dog to feed her three children.

George Donner's wound from fixing the axle became worse. It was infected. Eliza Donner watched as her mother bathed it, trying to clean it. But it did no good. The infection grew worse and his hand became inflamed and swollen. He had no energy left.

In the camp above, the survivors began to pull off the hides that had served as the roofs of their makeshift log cabins. Then they cut them up and boiled them, hoping for some nutrition, anything to fill their empty stomachs.

By the middle of January, the snow around both camps was higher than 12 feet. Things were beyond desperate. As the mounds of snow piled up, a group of the strongest men and women set out to find help. They had to do something. If they were going to die, they would die trying to find help for everyone. They called themselves "The Forlorn Hope."

The group fashioned snowshoes from small branches cut from nearby trees and strips of ox hide. They packed lightly, taking small bits of food, a rifle and a blanket each, a hatchet, and some pistols. Then they set out into the deep and drifting snow to find help.

The Forlorn Hope immediately found it was nearly impossible to climb the steep slopes covered by loose, powdery snow. After weeks of little food, they had no energy. But they pushed on anyway. Each one knew they were very close to death, and if they could not make it out, everyone in both camps would die, slowly and horribly.

The Forlorn Hope became lost and confused and soon had no food. They began to die one after the other. On January 12, 25 days after setting out, they stumbled into a Native American camp. They looked so emaciated and frightening the Native Americans took one look and fled.

The group continued on, into terrain so steep and rocky they had to pull themselves up by shrubs growing in crevices. They were battered and starving, their toes were black and their feet were swollen and bloody from repeated frostbite. Their boots and moccasins were falling apart, so they tied fragments of blanket around them.

One man went snowblind and could no longer see because of the harsh light reflecting off the snow around him.

Finally, the survivors stumbled down a hill and out of the snow. They were so hungry they started a fire and took apart their snowshoes. Then they toasted the rotted, leather thongs they had pulled off their snowshoes and ate them. Two men and five women made it to California to spread the word of the disaster in the Sierras.

Hurry back into the mountains, they said, before everyone in the Donner Party is dead! Thanks to efforts of the Forlorn Hope, three rescue parties set out from California into the High Sierras to bring out survivors of the doomed Donner Party.

That is when the troubled talk about the Donner Party began.

When the rescuers arrived in the mountains to bring people to safety, they found something unsettling. There was evidence that those who survived had eaten the dead.

The first rescue group left on February 4, but it was trapped by high rivers and deep snow. On February 18, another group set out. As they reached the cabins at Truckee Lake, a woman appeared from a hole in the snow and stared at them. "Are you men from California, or do you come from heaven?" she asked.

Rescuers found that 13 bodies had been loosely buried in snow near the cabins. Some of the survivors seemed to have lost their minds, babbling in ways that made no sense to the rescuers.

The relief party doled out food in small portions. They were concerned that if the starving survivors ate too much too quickly, it would kill them.

One boy, crazed with hunger, found the extra food and began to eat. He could not stop. By the time a man from the rescue party found him, he was dead. The boy's weak body could not take the sudden rush of energy from so much food after so much time without eating.

All the cabins were buried in snow. What was left of the ox-hide roofs on the cabins in Truckee Lake were so sodden they had begun to rot. The foul smell was overpowering. Three men from the rescue party trekked to the Donner camp and brought back four gaunt children and three adults.

Rescuers decided they would take the weakest of the survivors first, thinking that they could return later and get the others. They did not understand how weak and near death everyone was. The picked out 23 people to bring to the safety of California first, leaving 21 in the cabins at Truckee Lake and 12 at Alder Creek. It wasn't until March 3 that a third and final rescue party arrived back at the camps.

What they found would fan the flames of controversy about how the Donner Party had survived.

One of the survivors, perhaps insane from the ordeal, told them she had considered eating a man who had died earlier. Later, the rescuers found the man's mutilated body. It looked as if pieces of his shoulder had been cut out.

At Alder Creek, two rescuers said they saw a survivor run off carrying a human leg. He threw it into a hole when he saw them. The leg had belonged to Jacob Donner.

Two rescuers claimed they found a pot of what looked like human stew simmering in one of the disintegrating cabins at Truckee Lake.

George Donner was too weak to travel. His hand was so gangrenous that he could not move. His wife refused to leave him. They both died in the mountains, so close to freedom and their dream of California.

In the end, of the 87 people who entered the Wasatch Mountains with George Donner, only 48 made it to California. Eliza Donner and her brothers and sisters were among the ones to survive.

Eliza Donner spent the rest of her life defending her father's reputation. She told anyone who listened that the snow was too deep to get to any bodies. She said the stories were lies, made up by men looking for attention.

Despite her tragic trip to California, Eliza Donner lived a long and happy life. When she was older, she wrote of that terrible time in the Sierra Nevada Mountains. She wrote lovingly of her father. She would say that she was "indignant" that anyone dared mention her father and "acts of brutality, inhumanity, and cannibalism" in the same sentence.

Eliza Donner said her parents had given their lives and their last bits of food to allow others to live.

It did no good. The stories were far too sensational. The argument over whether the Donner Party resorted to cannibalism continues today.

WHAT ELSE IS GOING ON IN 1846?

- While being rung for George Washington's birthday, the Liberty Bell in Philadelphia acquires the famous crack that stopped it from ringing.

- The Mexican-American war begins on several fronts, with Texas border disputes and California declaring independence from Mexico.

- Adolphe Sax invents and patents the saxophone.

- Iowa is admitted as the 29th state in the United States of America.

adrift: floating aimlessly without power.

Antarctic Circle: an imaginary circle that extends north about 1,620 miles in every direction from the South Pole.

Antarctica: the land around the South Pole that is one of the seven continents.

bail: to clear water from a boat.

barren: bare land with poor soil and few plants.

biologist: a scientist who studies life and living things.

blubber: a thick layer of fat under a sea mammal's skin.

cannibal: an animal that eats its own species.

canyon: a deep, narrow valley with steep sides.

chart: a map or detailed plan.

cholera: a short-lasting, often fatal disease caused by bacteria in dirty water, milk, or food.

civilized: polite, with good manners.

clique: a group that excludes people not in the group.

compass: a device that uses a magnet to show which direction is north.

colony: an area controlled by or belonging to another country.

contagious: easy to catch.

continent: one of the earth's large landmasses, including Africa, Antarctica, Australia, North America, South America, and Asia and Europe (called Eurasia).

current: the steady flow of water in one direction.

desiccated: dried up.

desolate: a place without any people.

encampment: a place where a large group camps.

endure: to experience something difficult for a long time.

eternity: forever.

expedition: a difficult or long trip taken by a group of people for exploration, scientific research, or war.

fertile: good for growing crops.

floes: large, flat pieces of sea ice.

ford: to cross a river.

formidable: large, powerful, and difficult to defeat.

friction: the rubbing of one object against another.

frontier: the land or territory that is the farthest part of a country's settled areas.

frostbite: damage to exposed skin that freezes from very cold temperatures.

gangrenous: when flesh dies from a wound.

geography: the features of a place, such as mountains and rivers.

glacier: an enormous mass of ice and snow.

gold nugget: a small lump or chunk of gold.

gorge: to eat large amounts of food quickly and greedily.

hazardous: risky or dangerous.

homestead: the home and land of a family.

horizon: the line in the distance where the land or sea seems to meet the sky.

pack ice: sea ice formed into a messy mass by the crushing together of floes.

inhospitable: describes a place without shelter, water, or food.

journey: a trip from one place to another.

landscape: a large area of land with specific features.

meager: very little, not nearly enough.

meteorologist: a scientist who studies and forecasts climate and weather.

mirage: something that is not as it seems, such as seeing water in the distance in the desert.

mourn: to show sadness about someone's death.

mutiny: a rebellion of a ship's crew against its captain.

nauseating: something that makes you want to vomit.

navigator: a person who works to find or direct a travel route.

negativity: being negative.

nutrition: the things in food that your body uses to stay healthy and grow.

oblivion: being forgotten.

ominously: in a threatening way.

parched: dried out.

physicist: a scientist who studies energy and matter.

pioneer: one of the first to settle in a new land.

polar: the cold climate zones near the North Pole and South Pole.

prairie: the wide, rolling land covered in grasses west of the Mississippi River.

precipice: a very steep or overhanging place, such as the face of a cliff.

rebel: to fight against authority or someone fighting against authority.

reinforced: made stronger.

salvation: saved or delivered from danger or difficulty.

savage: fierce, uncontrolled, and ferocious.

sextant: an instrument used for navigation at sea.

species: a group of plants or animals that are closely related and produce offspring.

spellbound: enchanted or charmed.

tether: a rope or chain that holds something close.

tiller: a lever of wood used to steer a boat.

trek: a trip that involving difficulties or complex organization.

wreathed: circled around something.

Boy Scouts of America Awards:
meritbadge.org

Aimed at providing resources for Boy Scouts earning their merit badges, this website has a wealth of tips! Search "wilderness survival" for good information and a free workbook.

Shackleton's Antarctic Adventure:
main.wgbh.org/imax/shackleton

Can't stop thinking about "Escape From the Ice?" Check out this dramatic 2001 documentary, narrated by Kevin Spacey.

National Park Service:
nps.gov

If you're feeling the call of the wild, go to a National Park—but be prepared! The National Parks Service is a good resource to connect you to national parks all over the country, with guides to make sure that you can explore our natural wonders safely and responsibly.

The Donner Party:
donnerpartydiary.com

Read clips from letters and diaries written by members of the Donner Party during their doomed expedition.

Lots of other lambs had been born in the same field as Little Lamb, but each one was different—some were black all over, some were white all over, and some were a mixture. Little Lamb was mostly white, but she had lovely black ears, a black nose, and black feet so it looked like she was wearing socks!

All the other lambs were different sizes too, but Little Lamb was the littlest of them all. But, although she was small, she had a big heart, and wanted more than anything to be useful. She decided to set off around the farm to see what she could do.

That day, the sheep were being rounded up ready to have their woolly coats sheared.

"Please can I come too?" asked Little Lamb.

"Not yet," said her father, the big curly-horned ram. "You are still far too small to be sheared, you don't have enough wool. Run along and play, Little Lamb."

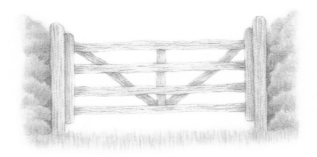

So Little Lamb went to see the big farm horse, who was about to take the farmer to market in the farm cart.

"Please can I help?" asked Little Lamb.

"Oh no," snorted the horse. "You are far too little to pull this great, big cart…"